Baby & Toddler Knits

LONDON, NEW YORK, MELBOURNE,
MUNICH, DELHI

Project Editor Katharine Goddard
Senior Art Editor Elaine Hewson
Managing Editor Penny Smith
Senior Managing Art Editor Marianne Markham
Producer, Pre-Production Rebecca Fallowfield
Senior Producer Katherine Whyte
Special Sales Creative Project Manager Alison Donovan

DK INDIA
Editors Janashree Singha, Manasvi Vohra
Senior Art Editor Balwant Singh
Art Editor Zaurin Thoidingjam
Assistant Art Editor Nikita Sodhi
DTP Designer Satish Chandra Gaur

First published in Great Britain in 2014
by Dorling Kindersley Limited
80 Strand, London WC2R 0RL

Material in this publication was previously published in:
Baby and Toddler Knits Made Easy (2013)

A Penguin Random House Company

Copyright © 2013, 2014
Dorling Kindersley Limited

2 4 6 8 10 9 7 5 3 1
001 – 193361 – Jun/2014

This edition produced for The Book People Ltd,
Hall Wood Avenue, Haydock, St Helens, WA11 9UL

A CIP catalogue record for this book is available
from the British Library

ISBN 978-1-4093-6968-4

Printed and bound in China by Leo Paper Products Ltd.

Discover more at **www.dk.com/crafts**

Baby & Toddler Knits

A handy step-by-step guide

Introduction

Baby and Toddler Knits shows you how to make gorgeous, custom-made, knitted pieces for a child. It provides you with the technical foundation, beautiful patterns, and all the design inspiration you need to create perfect gifts for newborns and toddlers up to three years old.

This beautiful book is suitable for knitters of all skill levels, whether you have only recently decided to take up the craft, or you have years of experience. With a selection of inspiring patterns, including clothing, toys, bits and pieces for the nursery, and accessories, there is something for everyone no matter what your personal taste or level of proficiency.

Throughout the book you are shown ways to experiment with different yarns, colours, embellishments, and fastenings. Have fun choosing the little details that make a design utterly unique to you. If you choose to substitute a yarn, refer to page 56 for a standard equivalent yarn weight chart. Select a yarn of the same weight and one that can also produce the same tension. Remember to knit a tension swatch before you begin a project and adjust your needle size, if necessary, to achieve the tension you need.

When creating anything for a baby or child, safety is paramount: make sure that small pieces are firmly attached and any ribbons and strings are securely fastened or out of reach. Remember to regularly check for wear and tear and repair anything that comes loose.

With *Baby and Toddler Knits* you'll find everything you need to knit with confidence and creativity so that you can make hand-knitted projects that will be cherished for years to come. Now the only difficult part will be choosing which pattern to knit first.

Contents

Newborn cardigan

THIS SOFT, LUXURIOUS CARDIGAN is perfect for a newborn baby. You only need to know stocking stitch for the body and garter stitch for the yoke, edges, and sleeves. Boys' and girls' buttonholes are worked on different sides, so follow the relevant instructions below. Choose a button to complement your yarn colour choice.

 ## you will need

size
To fit a newborn baby

materials
Rowan Cashsoft DK 50g in Sky pink (540) x 3
1 pair of 3.25mm (UK10/US3) needles
Stitch holder
Large-eyed needle
1 button

tension
27sts and 37 rows to 10cm (4in) over st st on 3.25mm (UK10/US3) needles

how to make

Back
Using cable cast on method, working between stitches, cast on 62sts.
Row 1 (WS): K.
Rows 2 and 3: As row 1.
Row 4 (RS): K.
Row 5: P.
Last 2 rows set st st. Cont working in st st until work measures 17cm (6¾in) from cast on edge, ending with a WS row.

Shape arms
Next 2 rows: Cast on 36sts, k to end. (134sts)
Cont in g st as set for a further 32 rows.

Shape right front
Next row: K57 and turn, leaving rem 77sts on a stitch holder.

Shape neck
Row 1 (WS): K1, skpo, k to end. (56sts)
Row 2 (RS): K to last 3sts, k2tog, k1. (55sts)
Row 3: As row 1. (54sts)

K 11 rows ending with a RS row.
Inc row (WS): K1, M1, k to end. (55sts)
K 3 rows without shaping.
Cont increasing at neck edge as set by inc row on next and foll 3 alt rows, then at neck edge of foll 2 rows. (61sts)
Next row: Cast on and k7, k to end. (68sts)
For a girl only:
Place buttonhole: K to last 5sts, cast off 3sts, k1.
Next row: K2, cast on 3sts, k to end.
For a boy only:
K 2 rows.
For boy and girl:
Shape underarm (RS): Cast off 36sts, k to end.
Row 1 (WS): K5, p to end.
Row 2 (RS): K to end.
Last 2 rows set st st with g st border.
Rep last 2 rows until work measures 16cm (6¼in) from underarm, ending with a RS row.
K 3 rows.
Cast off.

Shape left front

With RS facing, rejoin yarn to rem sts.

Cast off next 20sts, k to end. (57sts)

Row 1 (WS): K to last 3sts, k2tog, k1. (56sts)

Row 2 (RS): K1, skpo, k to end. (55sts)

Row 3 (WS): As row 1. (54sts)

K 12 rows without shaping, ending with a WS row.

Inc row (RS): K1, M1, k to end. (55sts)

K 2 rows without shaping.

Cont increasing at neck edge as set by inc row on next and foll 3 alt rows, then at neck edge of foll 2 rows. (61sts)

Next row (WS): K.

Next row (RS): Cast on and k7, k to end. (68sts)

For a girl only:

K 2 rows.

For a boy only:

Place buttonhole: K to last 5sts, cast off 3sts, k1.

Next row: K2, cast on 3sts, k to end.

For boy and girl:

Shape underarm (WS): Cast off 36sts, k to end.

Row 1 (RS): K to end.

Row 2 (WS): P to last 5sts, k5.

Rep last 2 rows until work measures 16cm (6¼in) from underarm, ending with a RS row.

K 3 rows.

Cast off.

Making up

Join side and underarm seams using mattress stitch (see p.58). Steam gently and attach the button.

A professional finish can be achieved with the right trimmings and embellishments. The colours in this understated mother-of-pearl button will blend well with anything.

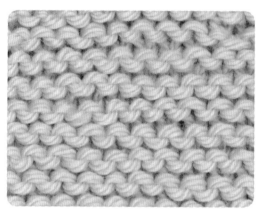

Garter stitch

(see p.39) makes a thick fabric. It is used here on the arms to help keep the baby warm, and also to provide an interesting variation in texture.

Stocking stitch

(see p.39) uses only knit and purl stitches and works well in this yarn as it produces a smooth fabric that looks store-bought.

top tip

The garter stitch edging keeps the stocking stitch from curling.

(See p.69)

Tiny tank top

THIS PROJECT, KNITTED IN STOCKING STITCH, can be worn on its own, or as an extra layer when it's chilly outside. Worked in a soft cashmere merino silk 4-ply yarn, it will make a great garment for either a boy or a girl depending on the colours you choose. It has ribbed edges with smart, coloured tipping to match the colour of the stripes.

you will need

size
To fit a child, aged 1 (2:3) years

materials
Sublime Baby Cashmere Merino Silk 4-ply 50g in
A: Vanilla (003) × 1 (1:2)
B: Sleepy (123) × 1 (1:2)
C: Paddle (100) × 1 (1:1)
1 pair of 3.75mm (UK9/US5) needles
1 pair of 4mm (UK8/US6) needles
2 stitch holders and spare needles
Large-eyed needle

tension
22sts and 28 rows to 10cm (4in) over st st on 4mm (UK8/US6) needles

how to make

Back
Using 3.75mm (UK9/US5) needles and yarn B, cast on 62 (66:70) sts.
Rib row 1 (RS): K2, [p2, k2] to end.
Change to yarn A.
Rib row 2: P2, [k2, p2] to end.
These 2 rows form the rib.
Work a further 4 rows, inc 2sts evenly across last row. (64 (68:72) sts)
Change to 4mm (UK8/US6) needles.
Work in stripe patt of [2 rows in yarn B, 4 rows in yarn C, 2 rows in yarn B, 4 rows in yarn A] throughout.
Beg with a k row, cont in st st until back measures 15 (17:19)cm (6 (6¾: 7½)in) from cast on edge, ending with a p row.

Shape armholes
Cast off 6sts at beg of next 2 rows. (52 (56:60) sts)
Next row: K2, skpo, k to last 4sts, k2tog, k2.
Next row: P to end.
Rep the last 2 rows × 3 (4:5). (44 (46:48) sts)**
Cont in st st until back measures 26 (29:32)cm (10 (11½:12½)in) from cast on edge, ending with a WS row.

Shape back neck
Next row: K12 (12:13), turn and leave rem sts on a spare needle.
Next row: P to end.
Next row: K to last 3sts, k2tog, k1.
Next row: P to end 11 (11:12) sts.
Shape shoulder.
Cast off.
With RS facing, place centre 20 (22:22) sts on a stitch holder, rejoin yarn to rem sts, k to end.
Next row: P to end.
Next row: K1, skpo, k to end.
Next row: P to end 11 (11:12) sts.
Shape shoulder.
Cast off.

Front
Work as given for Back to **.
Cont in st st until front measures 20 (23:26)cm (8 (9¼:10)in) from cast on edge, ending with a WS row.

Shape front neck
Next row: K16 (17:18), turn and leave rem sts on a spare needle.
Next row: P to end.
Next row: K to last 3sts, k2tog, k1.
Next row: P to end.
Rep the last 2 rows × 4 (5:5). (11 (11:12) sts)

Work straight until front measures same as back to shoulder, ending at armhole edge.
Shape shoulder.
Cast off.
With RS facing, place centre 12sts on a holder, rejoin yarn to rem sts, k to end.
Next row: P to end.
Next row: K1, skpo, k to end.
Rep the last 2 rows x 4 (5:5).
(11 (11:12) sts)
Work straight until front measures same as back to shoulder, ending at armhole edge.
Shape shoulder.
Cast off.

Neckband

Join right shoulder seam.
With 3.75mm (UK9/US5) needles and yarn A, RS facing, pick up and k24 down LS of front neck, k12 from front neck holder, pick up and k24 up RS of front neck, 6sts down RS of back neck, k20 (22:22) sts from back neck holder, inc 2 (4:4) sts evenly across the back neck sts.
Pick up and k6 up RS of back neck.
(94 (98:98) sts)
Next row: P2, [k2, p2] to end.
This row sets the rib.
Work a further 2 rows.
Change to yarn B.
Work 1 row.
Cast off in rib.

Armbands

Join left shoulder and neckband seam.
With 3.75mm (UK9/US5) needles and yarn A, RS facing, pick up and k70 (74:78) sts.
Next row: P2, [k2, p2] to end.
This row sets the rib.

Work a further 2 rows.
Change to yarn B.
Work 1 row.
Cast off in rib.

Making up

Join side and armband seams.
(See p.58 and p.60 for information on seams.)

top tip

Knit a tension square before you begin to make sure the tank top will fit correctly.

The shoulder seams are joined before the making up process. Join the right shoulder seam before you pick up and knit the neckband and the left shoulder seam before you pick up and knit the armbands.

For an elasticated fit the collar and armholes have a 2 x 2 ribbing (k2, p2 repeat). The stretchy edges make the tank top easy to put on and take off.

Join the seams using a discreet mattress stitch (see p.58). Try to match the stripes as closely as possible for a neat, professional finish.

This tiny bonnet sits against the baby's head, holding its shape with soft ribbing that is just snug enough to retain warmth.

Newborn hat

THIS QUICK AND EASY HAT IS DESIGNED TO MATCH the Newborn cardigan on pages 6-9 and Newborn booties on pages 18-19. It is sized to fit a newborn baby, but can be made bigger by using a thicker yarn with the appropriate needles. For example, try a different DK yarn with 4mm (UK8/US6) needles to make a hat for a baby aged three to six months.

you will need

size
To fit a newborn baby

materials
Rowan cashsoft DK 50g in Sky pink (540) × 1
1 pair of 3.25mm (UK10/US3) needles
Large-eyed needle

tension
25sts and 34 rows to 10cm (4in) over st st on 3.25mm (UK10/US3) needles

special abbreviations
rib: Work in rib, knitting all presented k sts and purling all presented p sts
rib2tog: Working in rib, k2tog

how to make

Pattern
Cast on 83sts using the cable cast on method.
Row 1 (RS): *K1, p1, rep from * to last st, k1.
Row 2: *P1, k1, rep from * to last st, p1.
Rep last 2 rows once more.
Row 5: [Rib 13, rib2tog] × 5, rib to end. (78sts)
Next row: P.
Next row: K.
These 2 rows form st st.
Work in st st for a further 17 rows.

Shape crown
Row 1 (RS): [K6, k2tog] × 9, k to end. (69sts)
Row 2 and every foll alt row: P.
Row 3: K.
Row 5: [K5, k2tog] × 9, k to end. (60sts)
Row 7: [K4, k2tog] × 9, k to end. (51sts)
Row 9: [K3, k2tog] × 10, k to end. (41sts)
Row 11: [K2, k2tog] × 10, k to end. (31sts)

Row 13: [K1, k2tog] × 10, k to end. (21sts)
Row 15: [K2tog] × 10, k1. (11sts)

Break off yarn, leaving a long yarn tail and draw this through rem sts twice. Use this end to join the back seam with mattress stitch (see p.58). Steam block lightly.

By tightly pulling the yarn through the stitches twice at the top of the hat, you will prevent gaps from forming in the future.

Flower headband

THIS FLOWER HEADBAND WILL KEEP HAIR out of your little one's eyes, or just act as a pretty accessory. It's so simple to knit you can have it completed in just a few hours. The flower-centre button can be left off the finished headband if you want a completely soft headband suitable for young babies.

how to make

Headband
Cast on 9sts in yarn A.
Row 1: K2, [yfwd, k2tog] x 3, k1.
Next row: P2, k5, p2.
K 2 rows.
Rep last 4 rows x 27 (29:31).
Cast off.

Outer flower petals
Cast on 10sts in yarn B.
Row 1: [Inc 1st] x 2.
Turn and work on 4sts just knitted.
Work 9 rows in st st beg with a p row.
Next row: K2tog, ssk. Lift first st on needle over second st. (1st)
*Next row: K1 into next cast on st, inc 1st.
Turn and work on 4sts on needle only.
Work 9 rows in st st beg with a p row.
Next row: K2tog, ssk. Lift first st on needle over second st.** (1st)
Rep from * to ** x 3.
K into first cast on st to complete final petal. (2sts)
Cast off 1st. Break yarn and pull it through rem st.

Inner flower petals
Cast on 10sts in yarn B.
Row 1: [Inc 1st] x 2.

Turn and work on 4sts just knitted.
Work 5 rows in st st beg with a p row.
Next row: K2tog, ssk. Lift first st on needle over second st. (1st)
*Next row: K1 into next cast on st, inc 1st.
Turn and work on 4sts on needle.
Work 5 rows in st st beg with a p row.
Next row: K2tog, ssk. Lift first st on needle over second st.** (1st)
Rep from * to ** x 3.
K into first cast on st to complete final petal. (2sts)
Cast off 1st. Break yarn and pull it through rem st.

Making up
Seam the two short ends of the headband together using mattress stitch (see p.58).

Join both the outer and inner petals into a circle. Place the inner petals onto the outer petals so that each inner petal lies between two outer petals. Secure the flower in place on the headband and stitch the button to the flower centre with cream sewing thread.

Practise your increase and decrease skills (see pp.43-51) to knit the undulating flower petals in this pretty two-tiered bloom.

🍃 you will need

size
To fit a child, aged 0–6 (9–12: 12–36) months

materials
Sublime Baby Cashmerino Silk DK 50g in
A: Gooseberry (004) × 1
B: Cheeky (048) × 1
1 pair of 3.75mm (UK9/US5) needles

Large-eyed needle
Sewing needle
Cream sewing thread
1 × 16mm (¾in) mother-of-pearl button

tension
23sts and 40 rows to 10cm (4in) over lace st on 3.75mm (UK9/US5) needles

top tip

The seams along the base of the booties sit flat for comfort.

The fold-down cuff is knitted as one long piece, then folded and stitched to create a casing for the ribbon. The cast off adds a wavy edge.

Newborn booties

THESE TINY BOOTIES CURVE GENTLY to follow the shape of a baby's foot, providing plenty of room for growth. Increases and decreases curve the booties as you knit. We've chosen a soft DK yarn and used smaller than usually recommended needles to achieve a firm fabric suitable for keeping tiny toes warm and protected.

you will need

size
To fit a newborn baby

materials
Rowan Cashsoft Baby DK
50g in
Sky pink (540) × 1
1 pair of 3mm (UK11/USn/a)
needles
1 pair of 2.75mm (UK12/
US2) needles
70cm (27½in) co-ordinating
ribbon, 3–7mm (⅛–⅜in) wide
Large-eyed needle

tension
25sts and 46 rows to 10cm
(4in) over g st on 3mm
(UK11/USn/a) needles

how to make

Booties (Make 2)
Using 3mm (UK11/USn/a) needles, cast on 37sts.
Row 1 (WS): K.
Row 2: Inc in next st, k15, inc in next st, k3, inc in next st, k15, inc in last st. (41sts)
Rows 3, 5, and 7: K.
Row 4: Inc in next st, k17, inc in next st, k3, inc in next st, k17, inc in last st. (45sts)
Row 6: Inc in next st, k19, inc in next st, k3, inc in next st, k19, inc in last st. (49sts)
K 16 rows, ending with a WS row.

Shape for toe
Row 1 (RS): K17, skpo, k11, k2tog, k17. (47sts)
Row 2: K17, skpo, k9, k2tog, k17. (45sts)
Row 3: K17, skpo, k7, k2tog, k17. (43sts)
Row 4: K17, skpo, k5, k2tog, k17. (41sts)
Row 5: K17, skpo, k3, k2tog, k17. (39sts)
Row 6: K17, skpo, k1, k2tog, k17. (37sts)
Row 7: K17, sk2p, k17. (35sts)

Shape for ankle
Change to 2.75mm (UK12/US2) needles and work as follows:
Next row (RS): K1, *p1, k1, rep from * to end.
Next row: P1, *k1, p1, rep from * to end.
Rep last 2 rows × 2.
Eyelet row: K1, *yon, k2tog, rep from * to end.
Next row: P1, *k1, p1, rep from * to end.

Work edging
Next row: (Casting off) *k2, pass first st over second so that 1st rem on RH needle as if casting off, place this 1st back on LH needle, rep from * until 1st remains.

Making up
Fasten off, leaving a long yarn tail. Join row ends with mattress stitch (see p.58) using the yarn tail from cast off edge. Fold over ribbed edging and catch to main bootie with a long running stitch. Thread ribbon through eyelets and tie in a bow. Sew a few stitches through the yarn and ribbon to prevent the ribbon coming undone.

Rattle ball

YOU DON'T NEED TO KNOW how to knit in the round to make this simple striped ball; it is knitted on straight needles and then joined together with mattress stitch. The contrasting colour stripes and rattle, sewn inside, make it of both visual and auditory interest to curious babies. Choose black and white yarns for even more contrast if you wish.

❧ how to make

Pattern
Cast on 6sts in yarn A.
1st row: (Inc 1st) × 6. (12sts)
K 2 rows.
Next row: [K1, M1] to last st, k1. (23sts)
Next row: K.
Next row (RS): K4, [M1, k3] × 5, M1, k4. (29sts)
Next row: K.
Leave yarn A at side and join yarn B.
K 2 rows.
Next row: K4, [M1, k3] × 7, M1, k4. (37sts)
K 3 rows.
Leave yarn B at side and use yarn A.
K 2 rows.
Next row: [K3, M1] × 11, k4. (48sts)
K 3 rows.
Leave yarn A at side and use yarn B.
K 2 rows.
Next row: [K3, M1] × 15, k3. (63sts)
K 3 rows.
Leave yarn B at side and use yarn A.
K 2 rows.
Next row: K1, [k2tog, k3] × 12, k2tog. (50sts)
K 3 rows.
Leave yarn A at side and use yarn B.
K 2 rows.
Next row: [K3, k2tog] to end. (40sts)

K 3 rows.
Break yarn B and use yarn A for remainder of toy.
K 2 rows.
Next row: [K2, k2tog] to end. (30sts)
Next row: K.
Next row: [K2tog] to end. (15sts)
Next row: K.
Next row: [K2tog] × 3, sk2p, [k2tog] × 3. (7sts)
Break yarn, thread it through rem sts and secure.

Making up
Prepare the rattle by wrapping it in a layer of toy filling about 2cm (¾in) thick, and winding a length of yarn round the "parcel" to secure the rattle in the centre. This is necessary to stop the rattle working its way to the edge of the filling when it is inside the ball.

Join the side seam of the ball using mattress stitch (see p.58), leaving a gap of a few centimetres (1in) for filling. Stuff the ball firmly and insert the wrapped rattle in the centre. Close the opening using mattress stitch. Weave in any yarn ends and cut.

Wrap the rattle in a layer of filling and secure it with scrap yarn. This will prevent it from moving around.

Be sure to line up your stripes in straight rows as you stitch up the seam using mattress stitch (see p.58).

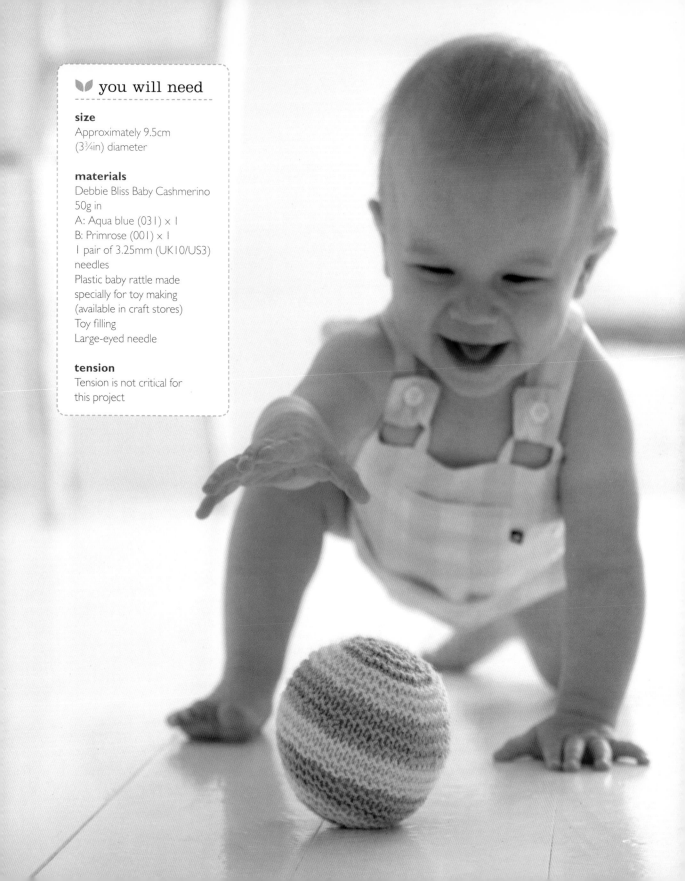

❧ you will need

size
Approximately 9.5cm
(3¾in) diameter

materials
Debbie Bliss Baby Cashmerino
50g in
A: Aqua blue (031) × 1
B: Primrose (001) × 1
1 pair of 3.25mm (UK10/US3)
needles
Plastic baby rattle made
specially for toy making
(available in craft stores)
Toy filling
Large-eyed needle

tension
Tension is not critical for
this project

Colourful bunting

A BRIGHT, FESTIVE ADDITION TO ANY ROOM, this colourful bunting is knitted using garter stitch. Knit the flags in colours to match your child's room. Choose as many or as few colours as you'd like, just be sure to adjust your yarn requirements if needed. Securely hang the bunting somewhere it cannot be pulled down by babies or children and cause a hazard.

 ## you will need

size
Length approximately
2.4m (94in)

materials
Rowan Belle Organic DK by
Amy Butler 50g in
A: Moonflower (013) × 1
B: Dahlia (029)× 1
C: Robin's egg (014) × 1
D: Clementine (020) × 1
E: Concord (035) × 1
F: Dew (025) × 1
1 pair of 4mm (UK8/US6)
needles
Large-eyed needle

tension
22sts and 30 rows to 10cm
(4in) over g st on 4mm (UK8/
US6) needles

 ## how to make

Ribbon string
Cast on 512sts in yarn A.
Now cast them off by knitting
2sts together into the back of the
stitches. Tie off yarn end and weave
yarn ends in neatly (see p.60, Darning
in an end).

Pendant flags
For the first flag, count 20sts from
the end of ribbon and then pick up
22sts (see pp.56–57).
Join in yarn B.
K 1 row.
Next begin pattern as follows:
Row 1: S1, k2tog, k to last 3sts,
k2tog, k1.
Rows 2–4: S1, k to end of row.
Rep rows 1–4 until 6sts remain
after 4th row.
Next row: S1, [k2tog] × 2, k1. (4sts)
Next row: S1, k to end of row.
Next row: S1, k to end of row.
Next row: S1, k to end of row.
Next row: S1, k2tog, k1. (3sts)
Next row: S1, k2tog. (2sts)
Next row: K2tog. (1st)
Cast off.

Making up
Break yarn leaving enough spare to tie
off tight and thread yarn through
large-eyed needle. Weave end in
neatly up the edge of the RS of the
pendant. Weave in the initial cast on
yarn end.

Now leave 3sts gap on your ribbon
and pick up the next 22sts. Repeat
previous instructions for this and all
subsequent flags. The repeating
colour sequence we've used here
is: yarns B, C, D, E, and F.

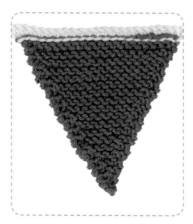

Pick up stitches from the same side
of the ribbon for each flag so the WS
is consistent across the entire length.

Diamond blanket

THIS IS AN IDEAL PROJECT for improving your knitting and purling skills. You don't have to follow any complex charts to create the attractive diamond pattern, you just need to be able to create basic knit and purl stitches. A double-sided moss stitch is used to border the blanket and prevent the edges from curling.

❧ how to make

Bottom border
Cast on 137sts.
Moss st row: [K1, p1] to last st, k1.
This row forms moss st.
Rep the row × 5.

Commence pattern
Row 1 (RS): [K1, p1] × 2, k4, *p1, k7, rep from * to last 9sts, p1, k4, [p1, k1] × 2.
Rows 2 and 8: [K1, p1] × 2, p3, *k1, p1, k1, p5, rep from * to last 10sts, k1, p1, k1, p3, [p1, k1] × 2.
Rows 3 and 7: [K1, p1] × 2, k2, *p1, k3, rep from * to last 7sts, p1, k2, [p1, k1] × 2.
Rows 4 and 6: [K1, p1] × 2, p1, *k1, p5, k1, p1, rep from * to last 4sts, [p1, k1] × 2.
Row 5: [K1, p1] × 2, *p1, k7, rep from * to last 5sts, p1, [p1, k1] × 2.
Rep rows 1–8 until work measures 84cm (33in) from cast on edge, ending with row 8.

Top border
Moss stitch row: [K1, p1] to last st, k1.
This row forms moss st.
Rep this row × 5.
Cast off in patt.
Darn in ends on WS and block according to ballband instructions.

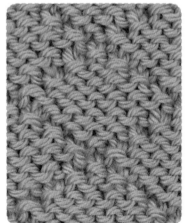

This subtle knit and purl texture adds interest. Very dark colours may disguise a great deal of carefully created detail, so try to choose a yarn colour that will show off your hard work.

The benefit of using a knit and purl stitch pattern is that the reverse side of the work will feature a negative relief image of the right side. This makes it double-sided – perfect for blankets.

A moss stitch edging is used to help the blanket to lie flat and also adds a soft frame to the finished piece. This edging is easy to create and looks very attractive.

Yarns

In its simplest form, yarn is made from combed fibres spun together for strength and durability. There are, however, numerous fibre mixes, textures, and effect yarns now available offering exciting creative possibilities to the hand knitter.

yarn weights

Yarns come in many different weights and thicknesses, which affect the appearance of an item and the number of stitches required to knit a sample tension square of 10cm (4in). Find the most suitable weight of yarn, according to the project, below. The yarn weight names give the common UK term(s) first, followed by the US term(s).

Yarn weight chart

What do you want to knit?	Yarn weight	Yarn symbol	Recommended needle sizes		
			EU Metric	Old UK	US
Lace	Lace, 2-ply, fingering	**0** Lace	2mm / 2.5mm	14 / 13	0 / 1
Fine-knit socks, shawls, babywear	Superfine, 3-ply, fingering, baby	**1** Superfine	2.75mm / 3mm / 3.25mm	12 / 11 / 10	2 / N/A / 3
Light jumpers, babywear, socks, accessories	Fine, 4-ply, sport, baby	**2** Fine	3.5mm / 3.75mm / 4mm	N/A / 9 / 8	4 / 5 / 6
Jumpers, light-weight scarves, blankets, toys	Double-knit (DK), light worsted, 5–6-ply	**3** Light	4.5mm	7	7
Jumpers, cabled menswear, blankets, hats, scarves, mittens	Aran, medium, worsted, Afghan, 12-ply	**4** Medium	5mm / 5.5mm	6 / 5	8 / 9
Rugs, jackets, blankets, hats, legwarmers, winter accessories	Bulky, chunky, craft, rug, 14-ply	**5** Bulky	6mm / 6.5mm / 7mm / 8mm	4 / 3 / 2 / 0	10 / 10½ / N/A / 11
Heavy blankets, rugs, thick scarves	Super bulky, super chunky, bulky, roving, 16-ply and upwards	**6** Super Bulky	9mm / 10mm	00 / 000	13 / 15

yarn labels

Everything you need to know about a yarn is on its label, represented by a symbol. Always keep the labels as they are vital for identifying the yarn if you run short and need more. New yarn needs to have the same dye lot number as the original purchase in order to avoid a slight difference in colour in the finished item.

 Symbols

Yarn manufacturers may use a system of symbols to give details of a yarn. These include descriptions of suitable needles and the required tension.

Yarn weight and thickness

4.5mm (UK 7/US 7)

Recommended needle size

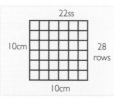

Tension over a 10cm (4in) sample square

50g

Nett at standard condition in accordance with BS984 Approx. length 115m (126yds)

Weight and length of yarn in ball

Shade/Colour **520**

Shade/colour number

Dye lot number **313**

Dye lot number

100% wool

Fibre content

Machine-wash cold

Machine-wash cold, gentle cycle

Do not bleach

Dry-cleanable in any solvent

Dry-cleanable in certain solvents

Hand-wash cold

Hand-wash warm

Do not dry-clean

Do not tumble-dry

Do not iron

Iron on a low heat

Iron on a medium heat

Knitting needles

Needles come in assorted types and are made of different materials, with various benefits when using particular techniques or working with certain fibres. Discover here how to choose the most suitable needles for the project you have in mind.

straight needles

Straight needles give a great deal of support to the hand when knitting. If you are new to knitting, start with these. Short needles are recommended for small projects; long needles are more suitable for wider knits, such as a baby's blanket, and for knitters who like to work by holding the needles underneath their arms.

Metal needles

When working with hairy fibres that may stick, slippery metal needles are great. If you find that you tend to knit too tightly, the slippery surface can help as it will cause a knitter's tension to loosen. Needles of more than 8mm (UK0/US11) in diameter can be clunky to work with, so are rarely available.

Bamboo needles

Bamboo is a lightweight, flexible material, and makes excellent knitting needles. It helps to keep stitches regularly spaced, creating an even knitted fabric with a good tension. Great for slippery fibres such as silk, mercerized cotton, and bamboo yarn. Recommended for arthritis sufferers. Thin needles will gradually warp with use to fit the curvature of your hand.

Plastic needles

For needles with a surface that is halfway between that of metal and that of bamboo, choose plastic. Plastic remains at a steady temperature during use, which may suit people who have arthritis. Avoid plastic needles of 4mm (UK8/US6) or smaller, as heavy projects may bend or break them.

circular needles

A flexible tube joins two needles to make a pair of circular needles. These come in different lengths and thicknesses. Choose a length that is most appropriate for your project: it should match the anticipated diameter of the knitted tube. For instance, a hat would call for shorter circular needles than a jumper knitted in this way. Knitting patterns usually specify the size required for the project.

double-pointed needles

The recommended option for socks, gloves, and narrow tubes. These needles are short and do not accommodate a large number of stitches. At first, some knitters may find that ladders form on each corner between the needles; however, this problem will disappear as you practise.

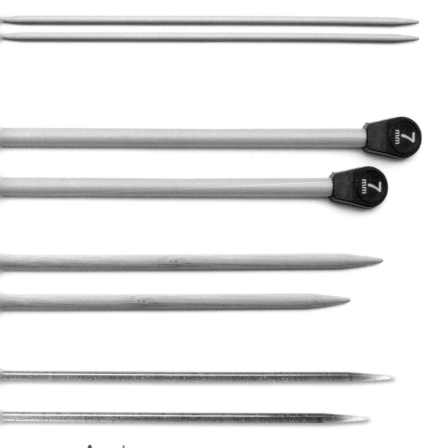

needle size

Knitting needles vary in diameter, from 1.5mm (¹⁄₁₆in) to over 25mm (1in). There are three common sizing systems: European metric, old British sizes, and American sizes. The chart, right, shows you how to convert between these systems. Needles are also available in various lengths to suit different projects.

🌱 Conversion chart

This chart gives the closest equivalents between the three needle-sizing systems. The sizes don't match exactly in many cases, but are the nearest equivalents.

EU	Old UK	US Metric
1.5mm	N/A	000 00
2mm	14	0
2.25mm 2.5mm	13	1
2.75mm	12	2
3mm	11	N/A
3.25mm	10	3
3.5mm	N/A	4
3.75mm	9	5
4mm	8	6
4.5mm	7	7
5mm	6	8
5.5mm	5	9
6mm	4	10
6.5mm	3	10½
7mm	2	N/A
7.5mm	1	N/A
8mm	0	11
9mm	00	13
10mm	000	15
12mm	N/A	17
15mm	N/A	19
20mm	N/A	35
25mm	N/A	50

Following patterns

Stitch pattern instructions are written or charted directions for working both coloured and textured knitting. Patterns can look daunting at first, but if approached step by step they are easy to understand. The following information can help if you get stuck.

understanding written instructions

Anyone who can cast on, knit and purl, and cast off will be able to work from simple knit-and-purl-combination stitch pattern instructions. It is just a question of following the instructions and getting used to the abbreviations. A list of common knitting abbreviations is given below, but for simple knit and purl textures all you need to grasp is that "k1" means "knit one stitch", "k2" means "knit two stitches", and so on. The same applies for purl stitches – "p1" means "purl one stitch", "p2" means "purl two stitches", and so on.

To begin a stitch pattern, cast on the number of stitches that it tells you to, using your chosen yarn and the recommended needles. Follow the pattern and work the stitches row by row and the pattern will grow beneath the needles.

The best tips for first-timers are to follow the rows slowly; mark the right side of the fabric by knotting a coloured thread onto it; use a row counter to keep track of where you are; and pull out your stitches and start again if you get in a muddle.

🌿 Knitting abbreviations

These are the most frequently used knitting abbreviations. Any special abbreviations in knitting instructions are always explained within the pattern.

alt	alternate	**p**	purl	**s2 k1 p2sso**	slip 2, knit one, pass
beg	begin(ning)	**p2tog**	purl next 2sts		slipped stitches over
cm	centimetre(s)	**(or dec 1)**	together (see p.49)		(see p.51)
cont	continu(e)(ing)	**patt**	pattern, or work	**st(s)**	stitch(es)
dec	decreas(e)(ing)		in pattern	**st st**	stocking stitch
foll	follow(s)(ing)	**pfb (or inc 1)**	purl into front and	**tbl**	through back of
g	gram(s)		back of next st		loop(s)
g st	garter stitch		(see p.43)	**tog**	together
in	inch(es)	**psso**	pass slipped stitch over	**WS**	wrong side (of work)
inc	increas(e)(ing)	**rem**	remain(s)(ing)	**yd**	yard(s)
k	knit	**rep**	repeat(ing)	**yfwd**	yarn forward (US yo;
k1 tbl	knit st through back	**rev st st**	reverse stocking stitch		see p.46)
	of loop	**RH**	right hand	**yfrn**	yarn forward round
k2tog	knit next 2sts	**RS**	right side (of work)		needle (US yo;
(or dec 1)	together (see p.48)	**sl k1 psso**	slip one, knit one,		see p.47)
kfb	knit into front and	**(skpo)**	pass slipped st	**yon**	yarn over needle
(or inc 1)	back of next st		over (see p.49)		(see p.47)
	(see p.43)	**sl k2tog psso**	slip one st, knit 2sts	**yrn**	yarn round needle
LH	left hand	**(or sk2p)**	together, pass slipped sts		(US yo; see p.46)
m	metre(s)		over (see p.51)	**[ ] ***	repeat instructions
M1 (or M1k)	make one stitch	**ssk**	slip, slip, knit		between brackets, or
	(see p.44)		(see p.50)		after or between asterisks,
mm	millimetre(s)	**s**	slip stitch(es)		as many times as instructed
oz	ounce(s)				

understanding stitch symbols and charts

As well as being written as abbreviations, for example "yon" or "sk2p" as shown opposite, stitch manipulations may be represented symbolically. Stitch symbols, usually laid out in chart form, are particularly helpful for understanding complex stitch manipulations such as lace and cables.

Stitch symbols

These are some of the commonly used knitting symbols. Any unusual symbols will be explained in the pattern. Symbols can vary, so follow the explanations in your pattern.

☐ = k on RS rows, p on WS rows
⊡ = p on RS rows, k on WS rows
⊙ = yarnover (see p.47)
☑ = k2tog (see p.48)
⊠ = ssk (see p.50)
⊠ = sk2p (see p.51)
⊠ = s2 k1 p2sso (see p.51)

Charts

Knitting instructions for stitch patterns can also be given in chart form. Some knitters prefer working stitch-symbol charts because they are easy to read, and they build up a visual image of the stitch repeat that is quick to memorize.

Even with charted instructions, there are usually written directions for how many stitches to cast on. If not, you can calculate the cast on from the chart, where the number of stitches in the pattern "repeat" are clearly marked. Cast on a multiple of this number, plus any edge stitches outside the repeat.

Each square represents a stitch and each horizontal line of squares represents a row. After casting on, work from the bottom of the chart upwards. Read odd-numbered rows (usually RS rows) from right to left and even-numbered rows (usually WS rows) from left to right. Work the edge stitches, then work the stitches inside the repeat as many times as required. Some symbols may mean one thing on a RS row and another on a WS row (see above).

Once you have worked all the charted rows, start again at the bottom of the chart to begin the "row repeat" once more.

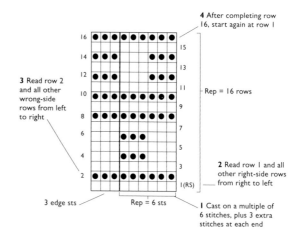

4 After completing row 16, start again at row 1

3 Read row 2 and all other wrong-side rows from left to right

Rep = 16 rows

2 Read row 1 and all other right-side rows from right to left

3 edge sts

Rep = 6 sts

1 Cast on a multiple of 6 stitches, plus 3 extra stitches at each end

measuring tension

Always knit a tension swatch before you start your knitting project in order to make sure that you can achieve the stitch size (tension) recommended in your pattern. Only if you achieve the correct tension will your finished knitted fabric have the correct measurements for the garment or accessory.

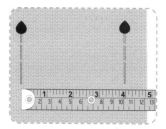

1 Using the specified needle size, knit a swatch about 13cm (5in) square. Mark 10cm (4in) across the centre of your swatch with pins and count the number of stitches between the pins.

2 Count the number of rows to 10cm (4in) in the same way. If you have fewer stitches and rows than you should, try again with a smaller needle size; if you have more, change to a larger needle size.

Key techniques

Learning to knit is a very quick process. There are only a few key techniques you need to grasp before you are ready to make simple items like baby blankets. The basics include casting stitches onto and off the needle, knit and purl stitches, and knowing how to correct simple mistakes.

knit-on cast on (also called knit-stitch cast on)

The knit-on cast on is ideal for a beginner knitter because it uses the knit stitch as its foundation. Keep all of your stitches on the left needle and knit in to the last stitch. Keep your tension loose during the cast on or your stitches may turn out to be too tight and hard to work when forming the next stitch.

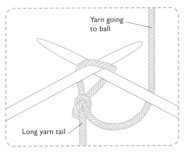

Yarn going to ball

Long yarn tail

1 Make a slip knot and place it on one needle. Holding the yarn in the left or right hand, place the needle with the slip knot in the left hand. Insert the tip of the right needle from left to right through the centre of the loop on the left needle.

2 With the yarn behind the needles, wrap it under and around the tip of the right needle. (While casting on, use the left forefinger or middle finger to hold the loops on the left needle in position.)

3 With the tip of the right needle, carefully draw the yarn through the loop on the left needle. (This is the same way a knit stitch is formed, hence the name of the cast on.)

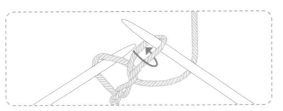

4 Transfer the loop on the right needle to the left needle by inserting the tip of the left needle from right to left through the front of the loop.

5 Pull both yarn ends to tighten the new cast on loop on the needle, sliding it up close to the slip knot.

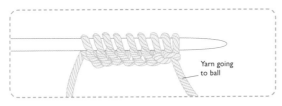

Yarn going to ball

6 Continue casting on stitches in the same way until you have the required number of stitches. For a looser cast on, hold two needles together in your left hand whilst casting on.

double cast on (also called long-tail cast on)

This cast on technique uses two strands of yarn, but only one needle; the resulting stitches are strong, elastic, and versatile. It is usually followed by a wrong side (WS) row, unless the reverse is the right side (RS). Start with a slip knot made after a long tail at least three times as long as the planned knitting width.

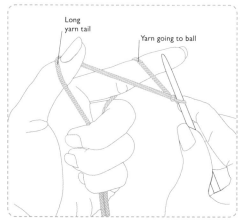

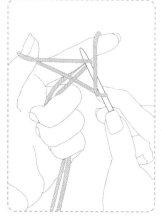

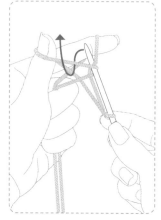

1 Make a slip knot on the needle, leaving a very long yarn tail – allow about 3.5cm (1⅜in) for each stitch being cast on. Hold the needle in your right hand. Then loop the yarn tail over the left thumb and the ball yarn end over the left forefinger as shown. Hold both strands in the palm of the left hand.

2 Insert the tip of the needle under and up through the loop on the thumb.

3 Wrap the tip of the needle around the loop on the forefinger from right to left and use it to pull the yarn through the loop on the thumb as shown by the arrow.

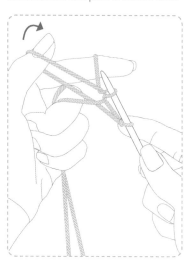

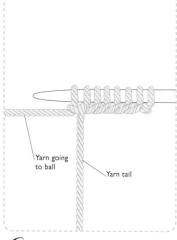

4 Release the loop from the thumb.

5 Pull both yarn ends to tighten the new cast on loop on the needle, sliding it up close to the slip knot.

6 Loop the yarn around the thumb again and cast on another stitch in the same way. Make as many stitches as you need.

casting off knitwise

When your piece of knitted fabric is complete you need to close off the loops so that they can't unravel. This is called casting off the stitches. Although casting off is shown below worked across knit stitches, the principle is the same for purl stitches. If instructed to retain stitches for future use, slip your stitches onto a spare needle or a stitch holder.

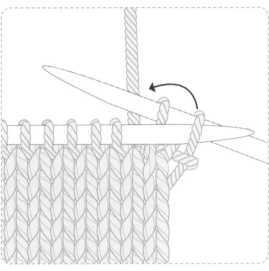

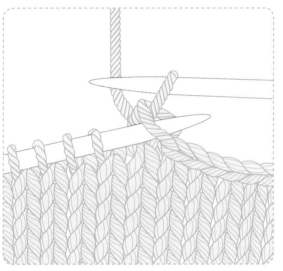

1 Begin by knitting the first two stitches. Then insert the tip of the left needle from left to right through the first stitch and lift this stitch up and over the second stitch and off the right needle.

2 To cast off the next stitch, knit one more stitch and repeat step 1. Continue until only one stitch remains on the right needle. (If your pattern says "cast off in pattern", work the stitches in the specified pattern as you cast off.)

3 To stop the last stitch from unravelling, cut the yarn, leaving a yarn tail 20cm (8in) long, which is long enough to darn into the knitting later. (Alternatively, leave a much longer yarn end to use for a future seam.) Pass the yarn end through the remaining loop and pull tight to close the loop. This is called fastening off.

three-needle cast off

Try using this technique to add interest to your project. This can be worked on the right side of the knitting (as here) to form a decorative seam, or on the wrong side.

Consider using a contrast colour to complement your project. An adaptation of the three-needle cast off may even be used to smoothly integrate pockets and hems.

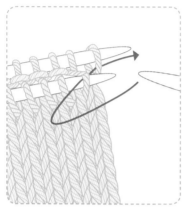

1 Hold the needles with the stitches to be joined together with the wrong sides facing each other. Insert a third needle through the centre of the first stitch on each needle and knit these two stitches together.

2 Continue to knit together one stitch from each needle as you cast off the stitches in the usual way.

3 When the pieces of knitting are opened out, you will see that this technique forms a raised chain along the seam.

slipping stitches off needle

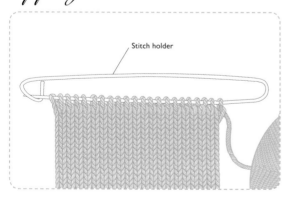

Stitch holder

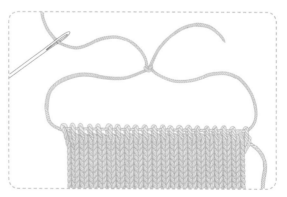

Using a stitch holder: If you are setting stitches aside to work on later, your instructions will tell you whether to cut the yarn or keep it attached to the ball. Carefully slip your stitches onto a stitch holder large enough to hold all the stitches. If you are only slipping a few stitches, use a safety pin.

Using a length of yarn: If you don't have a stitch holder or don't have one large enough, you can use a length of cotton yarn instead. Using a blunt-ended yarn needle, pass the yarn through the stitches as you slip them off the knitting needle. Knot the ends of the cotton yarn together.

knit stitch (k)

All knitting is made up of two basic stitches – knit and purl. Garter stitch (see p.39) uses only knit stitch. Try out fun stripes and different yarns in garter stitch to perfect your knit stitch. The odd dropped stitch does not matter while you're experimenting, put a safety pin through it so it does not drop further and sew it in later.

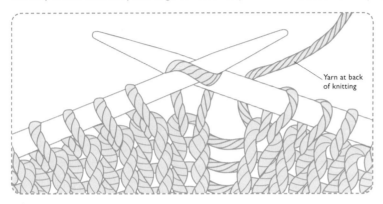
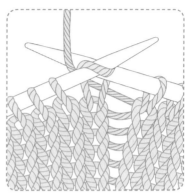

Yarn at back of knitting

1 Hold the needle with the unworked stitches in your left hand and the other needle in your right hand. With the yarn at the back of the knitting, insert the tip of the right needle from left to right under the front loop and through the centre of the next stitch to be worked on the left needle.

2 Wrap the yarn under and around the tip of the right needle, keeping an even tension as the yarn slips through your fingers.

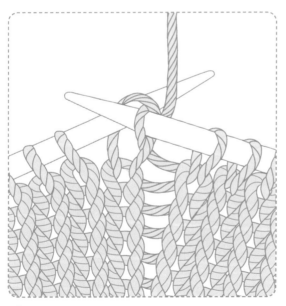

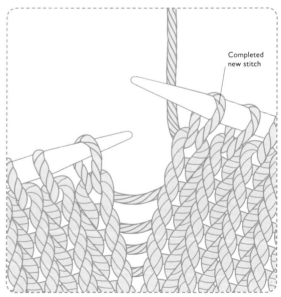

Completed new stitch

3 With the tip of the right needle, carefully draw the yarn through the stitch on the left needle. Hold the yarn firmly but not too tightly.

4 Let the old loop drop off the left needle to complete the knit stitch on the right needle.

purl stitch (p)

Purl stitch is a little more difficult than knit stitch, but like knit stitch it becomes effortless with practice. Once you are a seasoned knitter, you will feel as if you could work these basic stitches in your sleep. You may find your tension alters on purl stitches, so try holding your yarn a little tighter or looser to compensate.

Yarn at front of knitting

1 Hold the needle with the unworked stitches in your left hand and the other needle in your right hand. With the yarn at the front of the knitting, insert the tip of the right needle from right to left through the centre of the next stitch to be worked on the left needle.

2 Wrap the yarn over and around the tip of the right needle. Keep an even tension on the yarn as you release it through your fingers.

3 With the tip of the right needle, carefully draw the yarn through the stitch on the left needle. Keep your hands relaxed and allow the yarn to slip through your fingers in a gently controlled manner.

4 Let the old loop drop off the left needle to complete the purl stitch.

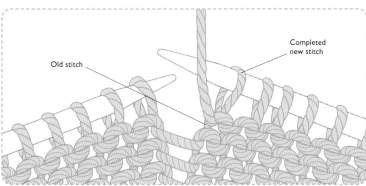

Old stitch

Completed new stitch

top tip
Garter stitch
creates a
textured fabric
that hangs flat.

basic knit and purl stitches

Once you know how to work knit and purl stitches with ease, you will be able to work the most frequently used stitch patterns – garter stitch, stocking stitch, and single ribbing. Stocking stitch is commonly used for plain knitted items, as in the Ballet wrap cardigan, left, and garter stitch and single ribbing for garment edging.

Garter stitch (g st)

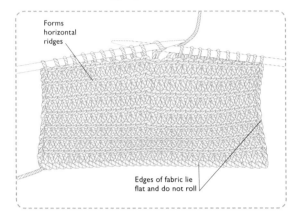

Forms horizontal ridges

Edges of fabric lie flat and do not roll

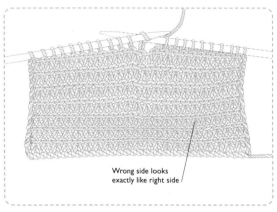

Wrong side looks exactly like right side

Knit right-side (RS) rows: Garter stitch is the easiest of all knitted fabrics as all rows are worked in knit stitches. When the right side of the fabric is facing you, knit all the stitches in the row.

Knit wrong-side (WS) rows: When the wrong side of the fabric is facing you, knit all the stitches in the row. The resulting fabric is soft, textured, and slightly stretchy.

Stocking stitch (st st)

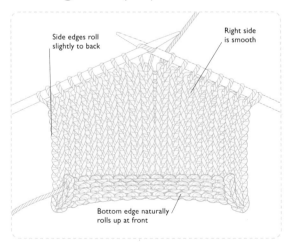

Side edges roll slightly to back

Right side is smooth

Bottom edge naturally rolls up at front

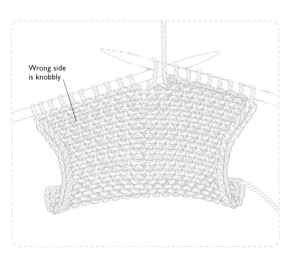

Wrong side is knobbly

Knit right-side (RS) rows: Stocking stitch is formed by working alternate rows of knit and purl stitches. When the right side is facing you, knit all the stitches in the row.

Purl wrong-side (WS) rows: When the wrong side is facing you, purl all the stitches in the row. The wrong side is often referred to as the "purl side" of the knitting.

Single ribbing (k1, p1 rib)

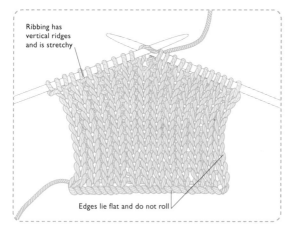

Ribbing has vertical ridges and is stretchy

Edges lie flat and do not roll

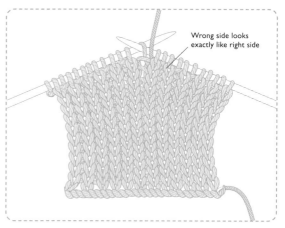

Wrong side looks exactly like right side

Right-side (RS) rows: Single ribbing is formed by working alternate knit and purl stitches. After a knit stitch, take the yarn to the front of the knitting to purl the next stitch. After a purl stitch, take the yarn to the back to knit the next stitch.

Wrong-side (WS) rows: On the wrong-side rows, knit all the knit stitches that are facing you and purl all the purl stitches. Work the following rows in the same way to form thin columns of alternating single knit and purl stitches.

correcting mistakes

These useful techniques will help you to complete your work if you run into any problems. The best thing to do if you make a mistake in your knitting is to unravel it back to the mistake by unpicking the stitches one by one. If you drop a stitch, be sure to pick it up quickly before it comes undone right back to the cast on edge.

Unpicking a knit row

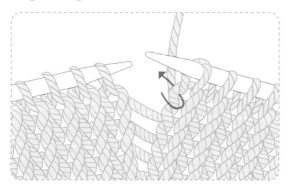

Hold the needle with the stitches in your right hand. To unpick each stitch individually, insert the tip of the left needle from front to back through the stitch below the first knit stitch on the right needle, then drop the old knit stitch off the needle and pull out the loop.

Unpicking a purl row

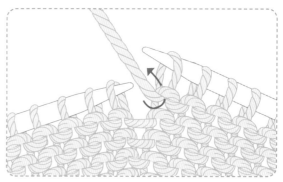

Hold the needle with the stitches in your right hand. Unpick each purl stitch individually with the tip of the left needle in the same way as for the knit stitch.

Picking up a dropped stitch

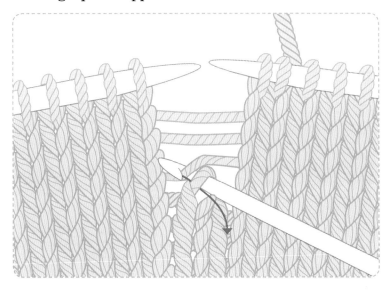

If you drop a stitch on stocking stitch, you can easily reclaim it with a crochet hook. With the right side of the knitting facing you, insert the hook through the dropped loop. Catch the strand between the stitches and pull a loop through the loop on the hook. Continue up the rows in this way until you reach the top. Then slip the stitch back onto your needle.

Picking up and working a missed yarnover in lace knitting and increasing

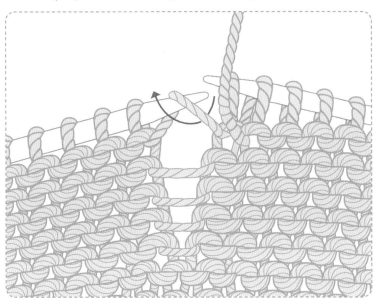

Count your stitches often when knitting lace to make sure you have the right number of stitches. If you are missing a stitch you may have left out a yarnover. There is no need to undo stitches all the way back to the mistake. Simply work to the position of the missing yarnover on the following row, then insert the left needle from front to back under the strand between the stitch just worked and the next stitch on the left needle (see left). Work this stitch through the front of the loop in the usual way, shown as purl in this example.

Understanding written instructions

Some stitch patterns will call for "slipping" stitches and knitting "through the back of the loop". These useful techniques are given next as a handy reference when you are consulting the abbreviations list on page 30.

Slipping stitches purlwise

1 Always slip stitches purlwise, for example when slipping stitches onto a stitch holder, unless instructed otherwise. Insert the tip of the right needle from right to left through the front of the loop on the left needle.

2 Slide the stitch onto the right needle and off the left needle without working it. The slipped stitch now sits on the right needle with the right side of the loop at the front just like the worked stitches next to it.

Slipping stitches knitwise

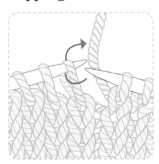

1 Slip stitches knitwise only if instructed to do so or if working decreases (see pp.48–51), as it twists the stitch. First insert the tip of the right needle from left to right through the front of the loop on the left needle.

2 Slide the stitch onto the right needle and off the left needle without working it. The slipped stitch now sits on the right needle with the left side of the loop at the front of the needle unlike the worked stitches next to it.

Knitting through back of loop (k1 tbl)

1 When row instructions say "k1 tbl" (knit one through the back of the loop), insert the right needle from right to left through the side of the stitch behind the left needle (called the back of the loop).

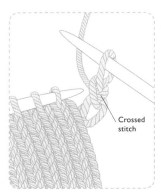

Crossed stitch

2 Wrap the yarn around the tip of the right needle and complete the knit stitch in the usual way. This twists the stitch in the row below so that the legs of the stitch cross at the base. (The same principle applies for working p1 tbl, k2tog tbl, and p2tog tbl.)

Increases and decreases

Increasing or decreasing the number of stitches on the needle is the way knitting is shaped, changing the edges from straight to curves and slants. Increases and decreases are also used in combinations with knit and purl stitches to form interesting textures and effects, including lace.

simple increases

The following techniques are simple increases used for shaping knitting. They create one extra stitch without creating a visible hole and are called invisible increases.

Multiple increases, which add more than one extra stitch, are used less frequently and are always explained fully in the knitting pattern.

Knit into front and back of stitch (kfb or inc 1)

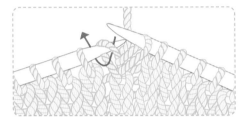
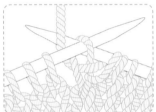
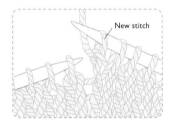

New stitch

1 Knit the next stitch, leaving the stitch being worked on the left needle. Insert the right needle through the back of the loop from right to left. This popular invisible increase for a knit row is also called a bar increase because it creates a little bar between the stitches.

2 Wrap the yarn around the tip of the right needle, draw the yarn through the loop to form the second stitch and drop the old stitch off the left needle.

3 Knitting into the front and the back of the stitch creates two stitches out of one and increases one stitch in the row.

Purl into front and back of stitch (pfb or inc 1)

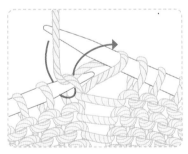

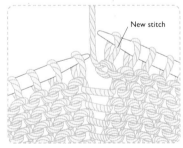

New stitch

1 Purl the next stitch, leaving the stitch being worked on the left needle. Insert the right needle through the back of the loop from left to right.

2 Wrap the yarn around the tip of the right needle, draw the yarn through the loop to form the second stitch and drop the old stitch off the left needle.

3 Purling into the front and the back of the stitch like this creates two stitches out of one and increases one stitch in the row.

Lifted increase on knit row (inc 1)

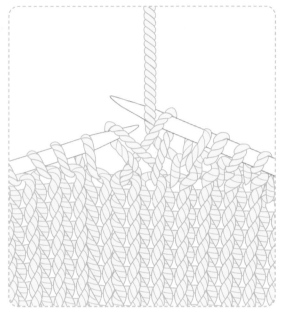

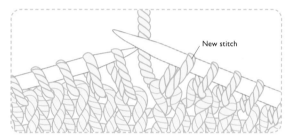

2 Knit the next stitch (the stitch above the lifted stitch on the left needle) in the usual way.

New stitch

1 Insert the tip of the right needle from front to back through the stitch below the next stitch on the left needle. Knit this lifted loop.

3 This creates two stitches out of one and increases one stitch in the row. (The purl version of this stitch is worked using the same principle.)

"Make-one" increase on a knit row (M1 or M1k)

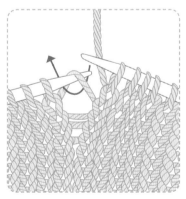

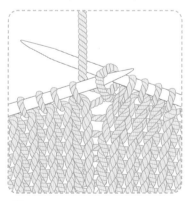

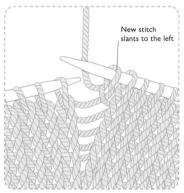

New stitch slants to the left

1 Insert the tip of the left needle from front to back under the horizontal strand between the stitch just knit and the next stitch. Then insert the right needle through the strand on the left needle from right to left behind the left needle.

2 Wrap the yarn around the tip of the right needle and draw the yarn through the lifted loop. (This is called knitting through the back of the loop.)

3 This creates an extra stitch in the row. (Knitting through the back of the loop twists the base of the new stitch to produce a crossed stitch that closes up the hole it would have created.)

"Make-one" increase on a purl row (MI or MIp)

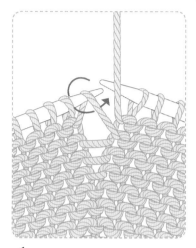

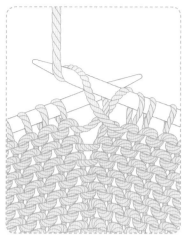

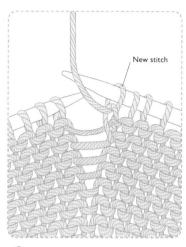

1 Insert the tip of the left needle from front to back under the horizontal strand between the stitch just knit and the next stitch. Then insert the right needle through the strand on the left needle from left to right behind the left needle.

2 Wrap the yarn around the tip of the right needle and draw the yarn through the lifted loop (known as purling through the back of the loop).

3 This creates an extra stitch in the row. (Purling through the back of the loop twists the base of the new stitch to produce a crossed stitch that closes up the hole it would have created.)

Multiple increases ([kI, pI, kI] into next st)

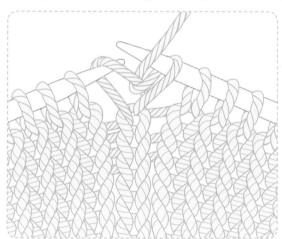

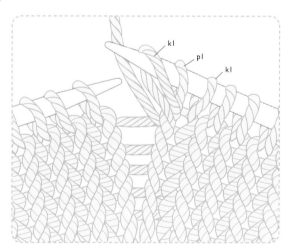

1 To begin the increase, knit the next stitch but leave the old stitch on the left needle. This is a very easy increase if you need to add more than one stitch to an existing stitch, but it does create a small hole under the new stitches.

2 Then purl and knit into the same loop on the left needle. This action is called knit one, purl one, knit one all into the next stitch. It creates two extra stitches in the row. You can keep alternating k and p stitches in the same loop to create more stitches if desired.

yarnover increases

Yarnover increases add stitches to a row and create holes, so are often called visible increases. A yarnover is made by looping the yarn around the right needle to form an extra stitch. Wrap the loop around the needle in the correct way or it will become crossed when it is worked in the next row, which closes the hole.

Yarnover between knit stitches (UK yfwd; US yo)

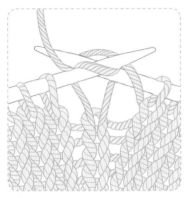

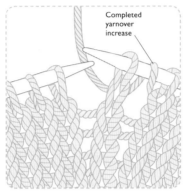

1 Bring the yarn forward (yfwd) to the front of the knitting between the needles. Take the yarn over the top of the right needle to the back and work the next knit stitch in the usual way.

2 When the knit stitch is complete, the yarnover is correctly formed on the right needle with the right leg of the loop at the front.

3 On the following row, when you reach the yarnover, purl it through the front of the loop in the usual way. This creates an open hole under the purl stitch.

Yarnover between purl stitches (UK yrn; US yo)

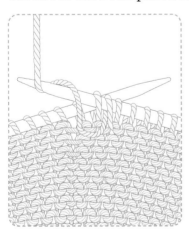

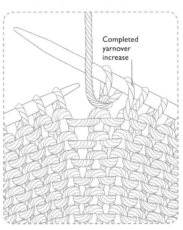

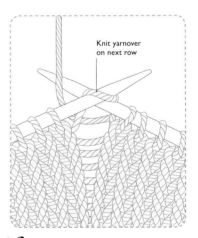

1 Bring the yarn to the back of the work over the top of the right needle, then to the front between the needles. Work the next purl stitch in the usual way.

2 When the purl stitch is complete, the yarnover is correctly formed on the right needle with the right leg of the loop at the front of the needle.

3 On the following row, when you reach the yarnover, knit it through the front of the loop in the usual way. This creates an open hole under the knit stitch.

Yarnover between knit and purl stitches (UK yfrn and yon; US yo)

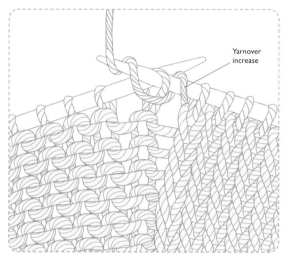

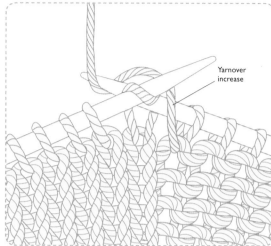

After a knit stitch and before a purl stitch (yfrn):
Bring the yarn to the front between the needles, then over the top of the right needle and to the front again. Purl the next stitch. On the following row, work the yarnover through the front of the loop in the usual way to create an open hole.

After a purl stitch and before a knit stitch (yon): Take the yarn over the top of the right needle and to the back of the work, then knit the next stitch. On the following row, work the yarnover through the front of the loop in the usual way to create an open hole.

Yarnover at the beginning of a row (UK yfwd and yrn; US yo)

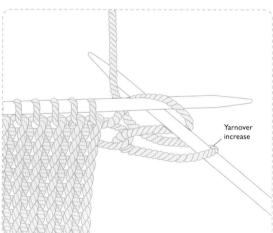

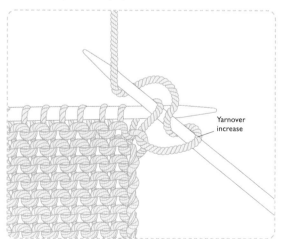

At the beginning of a row before a knit stitch (yfwd):
Insert the tip of the right needle behind the yarn and into the first stitch knitwise. Then take the yarn over the top of the right needle to the back and complete the knit stitch. On the following row, work the yarnover through the front of the loop in the usual way to create an open scallop at the edge.

At the beginning of a row before a purl stitch (yrn):
Wrap the yarn from front to back over the top of the right needle and to the front again between the needles. Then purl the first stitch. On the following row, work the yarnover through the front of the loop in the usual way to create an open scallop at the edge.

Closed yarnover on garter stitch

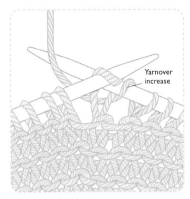

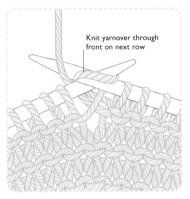

Knit yarnover through front on next row

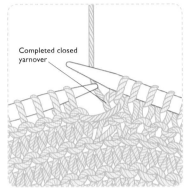

Completed closed yarnover

1 This is used as an "invisible" increase and is especially good for garter stitch. Take the yarn from back to front over the top of the right needle, then around the needle to the back of the work between the needles. Knit the next stitch in the usual way.

2 On the next row, knit the yarnover through the front loop (the strand at the front of the left needle).

3 This creates a crossed stitch and closes the yarnover hole. Although the crossed stitch is similar to the one made with a make-one increase (see pp.44-45), it is looser, which is perfect for the loose garter stitch texture.

simple decreases

These simple decreases are often used for shaping knitting and, paired with increases, for textured stitches. More complicated decreases are always explained in knitting instructions. Most of the decreases that follow are single decreases that subtract only one stitch from the knitting, but a few double decreases are included.

Knit two together (k2tog or dec 1)

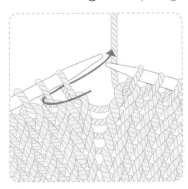

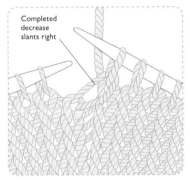

Completed decrease slants right

1 Insert the tip of the right needle from left to right through the second stitch and the first stitch on the left needle.

2 Wrap the yarn around the tip of the right needle, draw the yarn through both loops and drop the old stitches off the left needle.

3 This makes two stitches into one and decreases one stitch in the row. The completed stitch slants to the right.

Purl two together (p2tog or dec 1)

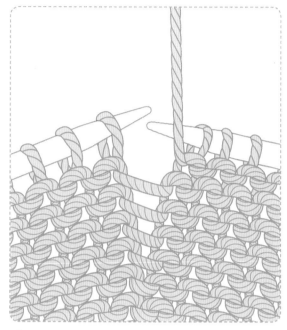

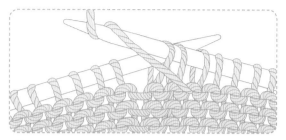

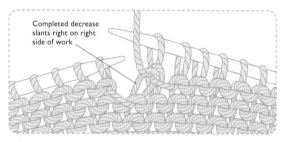

2 Wrap the yarn around the tip of the right needle, draw the yarn through both loops and drop the old stitches off the left needle.

Completed decrease slants right on right side of work

1 Use the p2tog decrease where a pattern specifies "decrease 1" on a purl row. Insert the tip of the right needle from right to left through the first then the second stitch on the left needle.

3 This makes two stitches into one and decreases one stitch in the row.

Slip one, knit one, pass slipped stitch over (sl k1 psso or skpo)

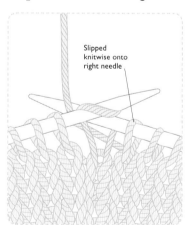

Slipped knitwise onto right needle

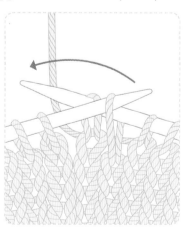

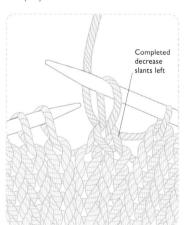

Completed decrease slants left

1 Slip the first stitch on the left needle knitwise (see p.42) onto the right needle without working it. Knit the next stitch.

2 Pick up the slipped stitch with the tip of the left needle and pass it over the knit stitch and off the right needle.

3 This makes two stitches into one and decreases one stitch in the row.

Slip, slip, knit (ssk)

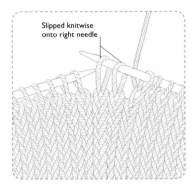

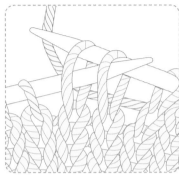

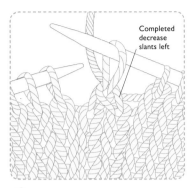

Slipped knitwise onto right needle

Completed decrease slants left

1 Slip the next two stitches on the left needle knitwise (see p.42), one at a time, onto the right needle without working them.

2 Insert the tip of the left needle from left to right through the fronts of the two slipped stitches (the right needle is now behind the left). Knit these two stitches together.

3 This makes two stitches into one and decreases one stitch in the row.

Slip, slip, purl (ssp)

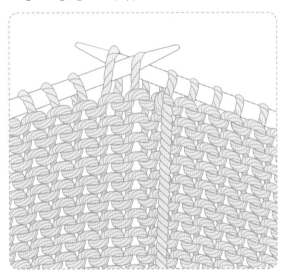

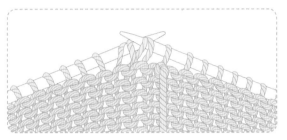

3 Holding the right needle at the back, bring the needle tip upwards from left to right through the back of the two stitches, bringing the right needle in front of the left as it comes through the stitches.

1 Keeping yarn at the front, slip two stitches, one at a time, knitwise (see p.42) onto the right needle without working them as for ssk decrease above.

2 Holding the needles tip to tip, insert the left needle into both stitches and transfer back to the left needle without twisting them.

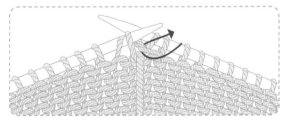

4 Lay the yarn between the needles as for purl. Take the right needle down and back through both loops, then slide them off the left needle together. This makes one stitch out of the two, and decreases one stitch in the row.

Double decreases

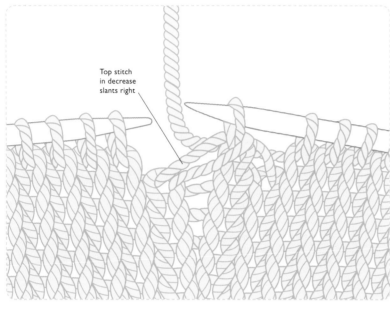

Top stitch in decrease slants right

k3tog: Insert the tip of the right needle from left to right through the third stitch on the left needle, then the second, then the first. Knit these three together. This decreases two stitches at once.

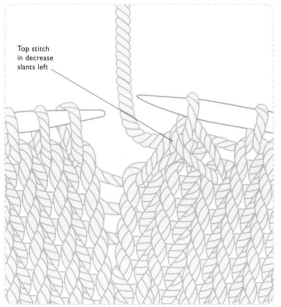

Top stitch in decrease slants left

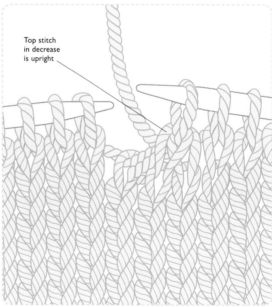

Top stitch in decrease is upright

s1 k2tog psso (sk2p): Slip one stitch knitwise onto the right needle, knit the next two stitches together, then pass the slipped stitch over the k2tog and off the right needle. This decreases two stitches at once.

s2 k1 p2sso: Slip two stitches knitwise together onto the right needle, knit the next stitch, then pass the two slipped stitches together over the knit stitch and off the right needle. This decreases two stitches at once.

Short rows

Short rowing, or "partial knitting", involves knitting two rows across some of the stitches, thereby adding rows in only one part of the fabric. It is popular for creating smooth edges in shoulder shaping, curving hems, and turning sock heels.

preventing holes

In most shaping applications, a concealed turn is required and there are two ways in which to work this: the "wrap" or "tie" and the "catch" are shown here.

Garter stitch, which uses only knit stitches on both RS and WS rows, does not require any wrapping.

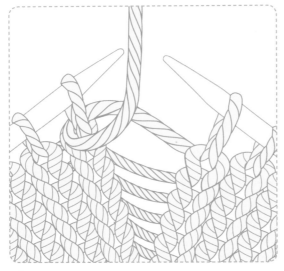

1 On a knit row: at turn position, slip next stitch purlwise onto right needle (see p.42), yarn to front. Return slip stitch to left needle, yarn back. Turn and purl short row. Repeat wrap at each mid-row turn.

2 On a purl row: at turn, slip next stitch purlwise, yarn to back. Slip stitch back, yarn to front. Turn and knit short row. Repeat wrap at each mid-row turn.

3 When working across all stitches on completion of short rowing: at wrap, insert right needle up through front (knit) or back (purl) of wrap. Work wrap together with next stitch.

Catch to close holes

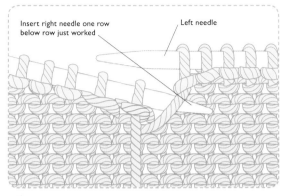

Insert right needle one row below row just worked

Left needle

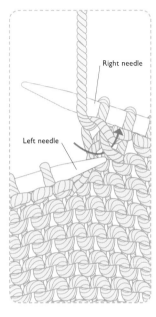

Right needle

Left needle

1 On either knit or purl rows, work a short row. Turn work, slip first stitch purlwise (see p.42), and work back along short row.

2 When knitting a completion row (knitting is shown temporarily reversed as this makes this step easier), insert right needle down through strand between first and second stitches on left needle as shown. Lift onto left needle.

3 Turn work again and knit picked up loop together with next stitch on left needle.

4 If completion row is purl, insert left needle upwards through the strand between the first and second stitch two rows below right needle. Stretch this loop, then drop it. Slip next stitch from left to right needle. Pick up dropped loop again with the left needle. Return slipped stitch to left needle. Purl these two together.

smooth diagonal cast off

This cast off is particularly suitable for neat shoulder seams on baby garments. This example assumes you are working a pattern with a diagonal edge to cast off in groups of five.

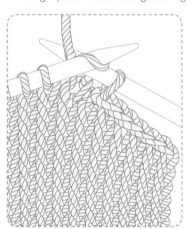

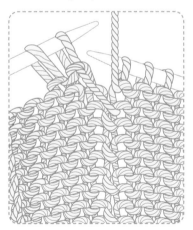

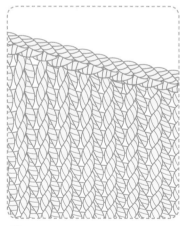

1 Cast off four stitches using cast off knitwise method, leaving the last stitch of the cast off on the right needle.

2 Knit to the end of the row on the left needle, turn the work and purl until there are only two stitches remaining on the left needle.

3 Purl these two stitches together. Turn the work. Repeat until the cast off length is completed.

Shaping: adapting a cast off shoulder to short row shaping

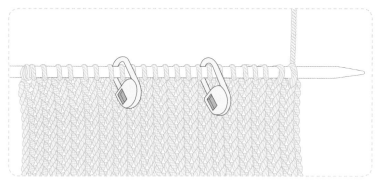

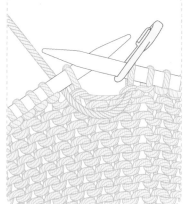

1 This shows adapting a stocking stitch pattern with cast off shoulder shaping. If the instruction is to cast off 8 stitches every alternate row, then 8 less stitches must be knitted every alternate row. The outer edge of a shoulder is lower than the neck edge, so short rows must be built up at the end of knit rows.

2 To practise this technique, work with a multiple of 8 stitches (24 stitches shown). Work the row with the first shoulder cast off instruction, but do not cast off any stitches. Turn work.

3 Purl to 8 stitches from the end and work a wrap (slip next stitch purlwise, yarn back, return slip stitch, yarn forwards). Turn and knit to end.

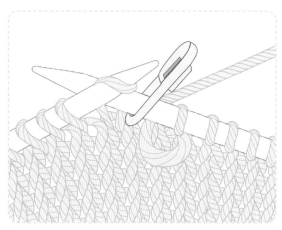

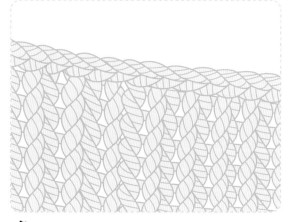

4 Turn work. Purl to 16 stitches from the end of the row, work wrap, and turn. Knit to the end (8 stitches on needle).

5 Turn work. Purl across all the stitches, picking up wraps by slipping them onto left needle and purling together with next stitch. Either cast off all stitches, or put them onto a stitch holder for grafting later. This gives you a smooth diagonal shoulder line. Grafting together two short row shaped shoulders makes an ideal seam for babywear.

Colourwork

If you like adding colours to your knitting there are a number of methods to use. The easiest is to knit using a multicoloured yarn, which changes colour along the strand. To add colours into the knitting yourself, you can work simple stripes, charted intarsia motifs, or Fair Isle.

simple stripes

Horizontal stripes are perfect for knitters who want to have fun with colour without learning more advanced techniques. There is an infinite variety of stripe widths, colours, and textures possible. You can follow any plainly coloured pattern and introduce stripes without affecting the tension or shape of the knitting.

Two-colour garter stitch stripe

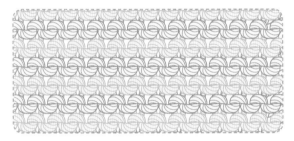

This stripe pattern is worked in garter stitch in two colours (A and B). To work the stripe, knit two rows in each colour alternately, dropping the colour not in use at the side of the work and picking it up when it is needed again.

Tidying the edges

When working two coloured, even row stripes, twist the yarns around each other every 1–2cm (½–¾in) up the side of the piece. Alternating the direction of the twist after each colour change prevents the yarns becoming tangled.

charted colourwork

The technique for charted stocking stitch colourwork opens up a world of designs. In intarsia, a separate length of yarn is used for each colour and the yarns are twisted together at the colour-change junctures. In Fair Isle, a yarn colour is stranded across the wrong side of the work until it is required.

Following a colourwork chart

The first step in understanding charted colourwork is to grasp how easy the charts are to follow. Rather than writing it out, your knitting pattern provides a chart with colours marked in symbols or in blocks of colour.

If a pattern covers the whole garment, a large chart is provided for each element with all the stitches for the entire piece. Where a pattern is a repeat, the repeat alone is charted. Each square on a stocking stitch colourwork chart represents a stitch and each horizontal row of squares represents a knitted row. Follow the chart from bottom to top.

The key provided with the chart tells you which colour to use for each stitch. All odd-numbered rows are usually right side (knit) rows and are read from right to left. All even-numbered rows are usually wrong side (purl) rows and are read from left to right. Always read your knitting pattern instructions carefully to make sure that the chart follows these general rules.

Finishing details

Finishing, as its name suggests, is the final stage of a project. Details that will make your knitting easier to assemble and look more professional, such as adding borders, hems, pockets, and fastenings, can, with a little planning, be incorporated into the actual knitting itself.

picking up stitches

Picking up edging stitches is a technique that even experienced knitters can sometimes find challenging. Careful preparation and lots of practise will help, though. It's worth trying it out on small pieces of knitting to perfect the technique before moving on to more important projects.

Cast on/off edge

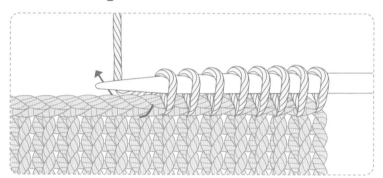

With RS facing, insert the needle in the first stitch. Leaving a long, loose yarn tail, wrap the yarn around the tip and pull it through, as if knitting a stitch. Continue, picking up and knitting one stitch through every cast on or cast off stitch.

Along row-ends

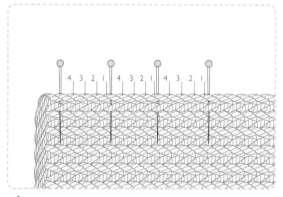

1 On light-weight or medium-weight yarn, pick up three stitches for every four row-ends. Mark out the row-ends on the right side of the knitting, placing a pin on the first of every four row-ends.

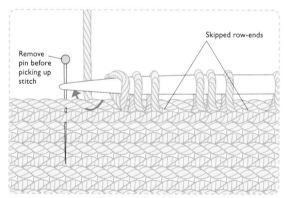

Remove pin before picking up stitch

Skipped row-ends

2 Pick up and knit the stitches as for picking up stitches along a cast on edge, inserting the tip through the centre of the edge stitches. Skip every fourth row-end.

With a crochet hook

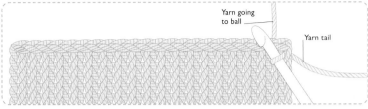

Yarn going to ball

Yarn tail

1 Use a hook that fits through the stitches. With RS facing, insert the hook through the first stitch, wrap the hook behind and around the yarn from left to right and pull through.

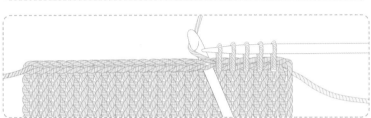

2 Transfer the loop on the hook onto a needle. Pull yarn to tighten. Repeat, transferring the loops to the needle.

Along a curved edge

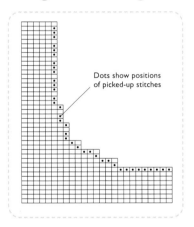

Dots show positions of picked-up stitches

1 When picking up stitches along a curved edge, pick up one stitch in each cast off stitch and three stitches for every four row-ends. Ignore the corner stitches along the stepped decreases to smooth out the curve.

2 Once all of the stitches have been picked up, work the border design as instructed in your knitting pattern.

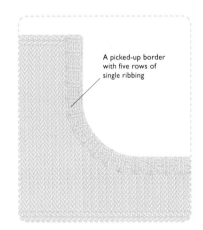

A picked-up border with five rows of single ribbing

🍃 Tips for picking up stitches

When picking up stitches use a matching yarn to hide picked-up imperfections. For a contrasting border, switch to the new colour on the first row of the border.
Always pick up and knit stitches with the right side of the knitting facing you, as picking up stitches creates a ridge on the wrong side.
Your knitting pattern will specify which needle size to use for picking up stitches – usually one size smaller than the size used for the main knitting.

After you have picked up the required number of stitches, work the border following the directions in your pattern, whether it is ribbing, moss stitch, garter stitch, or a fold-over hem.
If it is difficult to pick up stitches "evenly" along an edge, try casting it off again, either looser or tighter. If this doesn't work, pull out the border and try again, adjusting the number of stitches. Alternatively, try a smaller needle size if the border looks too stretched, or a larger needle size if too tight.

blocking a finished item

Before you sew up your finished project, it may need blocking. Always refer to your yarn label before doing this. Textured stitch patterns, such as garter stitch and ribbing, are best wet blocked or steamed extremely gently so that their texture is not altered – they should not be pressed or stretched.

Wet blocking

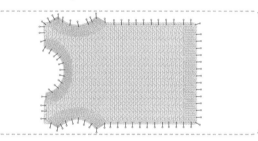

Wet blocking is best if your yarn allows. Use lukewarm water and either wash or wet the knitting. Squeeze it and lay it on a towel before rolling it up to remove more moisture. Pin into shape on another towel covered with a sheet. Leave to dry.

Steam blocking

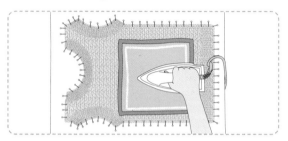

To steam block, pin the knitting to the correct shape, then place a damp cloth on top. Use a warm iron to create steam, but do not rest the iron on the knitting, and avoid any garter stitch or ribbed areas. Leave to dry completely before removing the pins.

sewing up seams

The most popular seam techniques for knitting are mattress stitch, edge-to-edge stitch, and backstitch. Cast off and grafted seams are sometimes called for and learning to graft open stitches together for a seamless join is very useful. Always secure the seaming yarn before you start.

Tips

Block knitted pieces before sewing together. After seams are completed, open them out and steam very lightly if the yarn allows.

Always use a blunt-ended yarn needle for all seams on knitting. A pointed needle will puncture the yarn strands and you won't be able to pull the yarn through the knitting successfully.

If knitting is in a fancy yarn, find a smooth yarn of a similar colour to sew up with.

It is better with mattress stitch to work with shorter lengths of yarn as long strands may break.

Before starting a seam, pin the knitting together at wide intervals. Secure the yarn to the edge of one piece of knitting with two or three overcast stitches.

Make seams firm but not too tight. They should have a little elasticity, to match the elasticity of the knitted fabric.

Mattress stitch

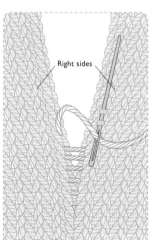

Right sides

1 Mattress stitch is almost invisible and is the best seam for ribbing and stocking stitch. Align the edges of the pieces with RS facing you.

2 Insert needle from the front through centre of first stitch on one piece and up through centre of stitch in row above. Repeat on the other piece, gently pulling seam closed every few stitches.

top tip

Join the seams according to the instructions in your pattern.

(For Newborn cardigan, see pp.6-9)

Edge-to-edge seam

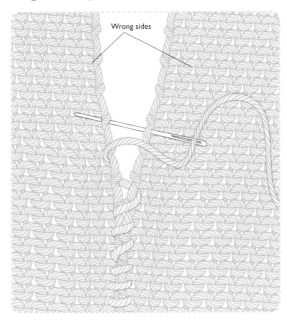

Wrong sides

This seam is suitable for most stitch patterns. Align the pieces of knitting with the WS facing you. Work each stitch of the seam through the little pips formed along the edges of knitting.

Backstitch seam

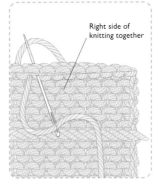

Right side of knitting together

Align the pieces with RS together. Make one stitch forwards, and one stitch back into the starting point of the previous stitch. Work the stitches as close to the edge of the knitting as possible.

Darning in an end

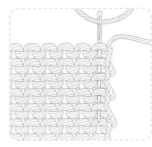

A piece of knitting has at least two yarn ends – at the cast on and cast off edges. For every extra ball of yarn used, there will be two more ends. Thread each end through stitches on the wrong side of your work.

Grafted seam

This seam can be worked along two pieces of knitting that have not been cast off or along two cast-off edges as shown here; the principle for both is the same.

1 With the right sides facing you, follow the path of a row of knitting along the seam as shown.

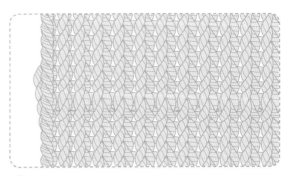

2 When worked in a matching yarn as here, the seam blends in completely and makes it look like a continuous piece of knitting.

fastenings and buttonholes

Choose an appropriate size and material for your project. Although nylon and plastic fastenings are lighter and less obtrusive, metallic or contrast-coloured ones can make a statement. Riveted press studs are useful; insert the shank between stitches and when connecting top to bottom make sure there are no sharp edges.

Attaching press studs

The male side of the stud goes on the inside. Decide position of studs by counting exact stitches and rows on each piece and mark positions with contrast thread.

1 Knot and sew in thread end at marker, catching half of each strand so stitches don't show. Place stud over marker and insert needle near hole just below the stud edge. Bring needle up through stud hole.

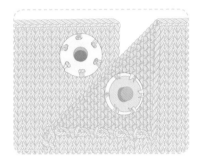

2 Repeat this three or four times through each hole, never taking the needle through to the right side. Move needle to next hole and repeat. To secure thread, sew two small backstitches, then sew a loop, thread the needle back through and pull tightly to secure thread.

Knitted button loop

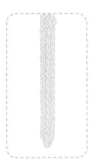

1 Using a cable cast on, cast on as many stitches as required for length of loop. Next row, cast off all stitches.

2 Fold the loop in half. Use the ends to sew the loop neatly and firmly to the inside edge of the item.

Open eyelet buttonhole (also used in lace patterns)

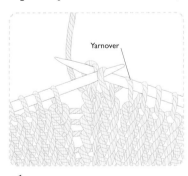

1 For an open eyelet on stocking stitch, work a yarnover on right needle. Work a "sl kl psso" decrease after yarnover.

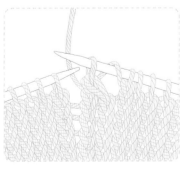

2 The yarnover creates a hole and the decrease compensates for the extra loop so the knitting remains the same width.

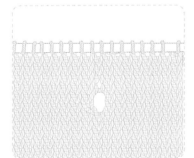

3 On the following row, purl the yarnover. Open eyelets can be arranged to create any number of lace textures.

Index

Acknowledgements

Dorling Kindersley would like to thank the following people for their hard work and contributions towards *Baby and Toddler Knits*:

Knitting designers Debi Birkin, Sian Brown, Fiona Goble, Zoe Halstead, Val Pierce, and Frederica Patmore

Knitters Brenda Bostock, June Cole, Antonella Conti, Sally Cuthbert, Joan Doyle, Eva Hallas, Dolly Howes, Brenda Jennings, Maisie Lawrence, Patricia Liddle, Ann McFaull, Karen Tattersall, Jane Wales, and Brenda Willows

Pattern checkers Carol Ibbetson and Rachel Vowles

Proofreader Angela Baynham

Indexer Marie Lorimer

Design assistance Charlotte Johnson, Nicola Rodway, and Clare Patane

Editorial assistance Katharine Goddard and Grace Redhead

Additional photography Dave King

Photography assistant Julie Stewart

Props George & Beth and Backgrounds

Location for photography 1st Option

The following yarn manufacturers and distributors for supplying yarn for the projects Coats Crafts UK, King Cole Ltd, Sirdar Yarns, and Sublime Yarns

About the consultant

Dr Vikki Haffenden has an active career in all aspects of hand and machine knitting and knitwear design. She is the co-author of Dorling Kindersley's *The Knitting Book* and the consultant on *Knit Step-by-Step,* and *Big Book of Knitting.* Her particular interest is the exploration of technical knitting for the design development of knitted textiles and garment shapes. Vikki holds a PhD based in commercial knitting and knitwear design research, and currently teaches in the department of Knitted Textiles at the University of Brighton in Sussex.